Animal feelings

SYLVIA FUNSTON

D1518860

WITHDRAWN

Owl

Owl Books are published by Greey de Pencier Books Inc.
179 John Street, Suite 500, Toronto, Ontario M5T 3G5

The Owl colophon is a trademark of Owl Children's Trust Inc.
Greey de Pencier Books Inc. is a licensed user of trademarks of Owl Children's Trust Inc.

Distributed in the United States by Firefly Books (U.S.) Inc.
230 Fifth Avenue, Suite 1607, New York, NY 10001

We acknowledge the generous support of the Canada Council for the Arts
and the Ontario Arts Council for our publishing program.

Cataloguing in Publication Data

Funston, Sylvia
        Animal feelings

(The secret life of animals)
Includes index.
ISBN 1-895688-81-7 (bound) ISBN 1-895688-82-5 (pbk.)

1. Animal behavior – Juvenile literature. I. Title. II. Series.

QL751.F86 1998   j591.5   C97-932603-6

Design: Julia Naimska
Cover Design & Page Layout: Mary Opper
Illustrations by Pat Stephens

Photo credits
Front cover, Frans Lanting/First Light; page 4, H. H. Geithoorn/Valan; 5, Michael Goldman; 6–7, E. A. James/First Light; 8, H. S. Terrance/Animals Animals; 9, Thomas Peterson/Tony Stone Images; 10, Frank Krahmer/Bruce Coleman; 11, Art Wolfe/Tony Stone Images; 12–13, Kim A. Bard; 14, Cynthia Moss/Animals Animals; 15, Wendy Shattil and Bob Rozinski/Oxford Scientific Films; 16, Johnny Johnson/DRK Photo; 17, Daniel J. Cox/Tony Stone Images; 18, 22, Stephen J. Krasemann/DRK Photo; 19, Tom Brakefield/Bruce Coleman; 20, Mark Hamblin/Oxford Scientific Films; 21, Michael P. Turco; 23, Martin Harvey/NHPA; 24–25, Stuart Westmorland/Tony Stone Images; 26, David M. Dennis/Tom Stack & Associates; 28, Erwin and Peggy Bauer/Bruce Coleman; 29, J. Ireland and G. Bradley/First Light; 30, Michio Hoshino/First Light; 31, Patti Murray/Animals Animals; 34, Dick Haneda; 35, Robert Kusel/Tony Stone Images; 36–37, 41, Dr. Ronald Cohn/The Gorilla Foundation; 38, Robert Maier, Animals Animals; 39, 45 (upper), K & K Ammann/Bruce Coleman; 42, B. Spremo/Toronto Star; 43, M. W. Larson/Bruce Coleman; 44, Don Ryan/Associated Press; 45 (lower), Stephen Kline/Bruce Coleman; 46, Renée Stockdale/Animals Animals; 47, Myrleen Cate/Tony Stone Images.

Printed in Hong Kong

A   B   C   D   E   F

Contents

Fuzzy Feelings

"Come here, I love you. I'm sorry. I want to go back!" wails Alex before his medical examination. He sounds afraid. But Alex isn't being seen by a doctor — he's at the vet's office. Alex (below) is an African gray parrot who has been trained to speak English. Unlike most parrots, who copy human sounds without knowing the meaning, Alex actually understands the words he is saying.

Alex is a special case — most animals can't describe their feelings in words. No one knows for sure what a dog feels when its owner returns home, but it looks and acts as if it's happy (see opposite page). So scientists study what animals do, and look for ways they are like us, to try to find out what animals might be feeling. They have found that bird and mammal brains have an emotion command center just like yours does. In one experiment, a researcher removed part of this command center from a rat's brain to see which emotions it controlled. The rat walked fearlessly up to a cat and nibbled on the surprised kitty's ear!

In this book, you'll meet animals acting as if they are afraid or happy, ashamed or sad, cruel or kind. These are words that describe emotions *we* feel. We don't know if animals feel the same things we do or for the same reasons. But they seem to have an emotional life, even if it is a secret one. What you encounter in this book might make you chuckle, or it might make you sad. It might even change the way you feel about animals forever.

The look on this dog's face and the way its body slumps over suggest a bad case of the blues. Even if the dog could tell you in words how it feels, there's only one being whose emotions you can be certain of, and that's you. But one thing is becoming increasingly clear. Thinking and feeling are closely related. So if an animal thinks, as many appear to, then chances are it also feels.

FEELING BAD

Very Scary

Koko the gorilla and Washoe the chimp have both used American Sign Language, or ASL, to tell their trainers that they are afraid. Koko has never seen a live alligator, yet toy alligators terrify her — unless their bottom jaws are removed. Scientists say that this must be an instinctive fear in gorillas. But instinct doesn't explain why Washoe is afraid every time she sees a dust mop. After all, dust mops haven't been stalking chimpanzees in the wild for millions of years!

Researchers have taught several gorillas and chimpanzees to communicate with people using signs from ASL, the sign language used by many hearing-impaired people (see below). The boy in the diagrams on the left is showing how to make the sign for "afraid" — the same one that Washoe uses to tell her keeper when something frightens her.

1.

2.

These cats seem to be sleeping peacefully, but next time you see a cat start twitching during a catnap, you'll know it might be chasing imaginary mice or birds in dreamland. Or maybe its dreams aren't happy or exciting ones. Do you think animals can have nightmares, too?

Maybe Washoe imagines the dust mop could hurt her, the way a child imagines monsters under the bed. Scientists know that Washoe's imagination is so vivid they can use it to keep her in line. All they have to do is mention an imaginary "bogeydog" whenever Washoe doesn't want to stop playing outside, and she scurries back inside.

If some animals can imagine scary things, do they also have scary dreams? When you dream, you're in a deep kind of sleep scientists recognize by the rapid back and forth movement of your eyes beneath your lids. It's called rapid-eye-movement, or REM, sleep. Some sleeping birds and mammals show the same patterns of brainwaves that your brain shows during REM sleep, which suggests that they dream just like you do.

When a pride of lions is threatened, it's usually the lionesses that defend it. So you'd hardly call a lioness a "scaredy-cat." Or would you? A researcher was studying lions in the Serengeti National Park in Tanzania. He found that many lionesses rushed to defend their pride, but the same few always hung back, letting their braver sisters tackle the intruders.

Fighting Mad

Many animals living in groups use aggression to make it clear where they belong in the group. Aggression is frightening — it's supposed to be. But when, say, two wolves fight, do they feel the kind of anger we feel when things are against us? Or is what they do an instinctive reaction to each other's signals? One researcher set up an experiment that was so frustrating, the dog he was working with finally tore the equipment to pieces. That sounds like one angry animal, but we can't tell for sure what the dog was feeling.

What about anger that springs from a strong dislike of someone? Famous biologist Konrad Lorenz spent years studying geese. Two ganders (male geese) that were brothers developed a dislike for Lorenz's assistant, Paul. After one of them was run over by a car, the remaining gander's aggression increased so much that he even tried to attack Paul in his car. And if Paul threw his jacket on the ground, the bird wouldn't stop attacking it until he was exhausted.

Siamese fighting fish live up to their name. But do they go looking for trouble? In one experiment, male Siamese fighting fish were kept alone in tanks. Each time a fish swam through a ring suspended in the water, an outside lamp switched off for a few seconds. The darkness turned the wall of the tank into a temporary mirror. When a fish saw its image in the mirror wall, it tried to frighten it away. Some fish swam through the ring to fight with their reflections hundreds of times a day!

Whenever members of the Ross-on-Wye rowing club in England take to the water, they keep a sharp eye out for a swan called George. George hates row boats. Canoeists and kayakers can paddle by safely. But as soon as George spies a boat with oars, he flies straight at it like a fighter plane with its sights locked on its target.

When a wolf challenges another for its place in the pack, they face each other snarling, with hackles raised and fangs exposed. Suddenly the fight erupts. Just as suddenly, it's over, when the loser rolls on its back showing its soft underbelly. It's like waving a white flag of surrender. Immediately, all aggression fades and the winner backs off.

Mirror, Mirror

Fear and anger are instinctive — they are necessary to make an animal act to protect itself in the face of danger. But some feelings are more complicated. Animals can feel ashamed or sorry for someone, or even tell a lie, only if they can put themselves in another animal's place. They have to realize what it's like to be in a situation, and understand that it's probably the same for another animal in a similar situation. You do this without thinking much about it, but do animals have this self-awareness?

One clue for us to an animal's self-awareness is its being able to recognize itself in a mirror. Most animals don't recognize their reflections as themselves — remember the Siamese fighting fish on page 10? But some animals do recognize their reflections as themselves. A researcher anesthetized chimpanzees who were familiar with mirrors. While they were asleep, the scientist put paint on

You were first able to recognize yourself in a mirror when you were between 18 and 24 months old. It takes chimpanzees a little longer to do the same — they don't know it's themselves they're looking at until they are between 28 and 30 months old.

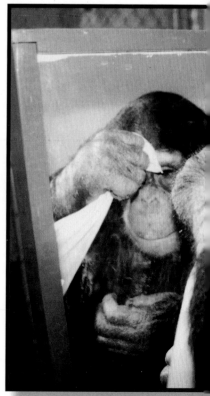

their eyebrows and ears. When the chimps awoke, they weren't aware of the dots until they glanced in a mirror. Immediately, they picked at the spots, then looked at their fingers. They must have known they were looking at themselves when they looked in the mirror. Why else would they check their fingers for paint?

There are many reports of chimps making faces at themselves or practicing blowing bubble gum in the mirror. Washoe the chimp looks in the mirror and says, "Me, Washoe," in sign language. Another chimp called Austin is fascinated by his video image, using the television to look down his throat, while his pal Sherman uses it to put on lipstick.

Seeing how animals act with friends and neighbors might also give us some clues about how aware they are of other individuals. Crows and other animals that live in small colonies seem to know each other. Some scientists think that the constant give and take of group living gives animals the skills they need to recognize and remember their companions. The same skills also probably help them to notice subtle differences in each other's appearance and behavior, which helps them read the mood and intentions of others. All these skills are essential for survival.

Seabirds that nest in colonies frequently pair up with the same mate year after year, even though they spend each winter apart. Is it each other they recognize, or their old nest site? To find out, researchers tagged birds with different colors so they could count how many partners found each other the following year. Then they made their old nest sites unusable. Kittiwakes obviously recognize each other because more than three-quarters of them ended up with their *old* mates on *new* nests.

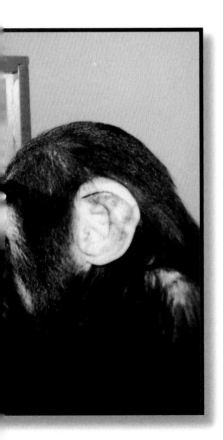

So Sad

Well-known researcher Jane Goodall has observed wild chimpanzees for many years, and she believes that chimps experience intense sadness when a relative dies. Flint, one of the chimps she observed, had a close relationship with his mother. She died when he was eight years old. After that, he stopped eating, avoided company and sat hunched over, rocking back and forth. As the days passed, Flint became more and more listless until, eventually, he died, too.

Two elephant researchers in Amboseli National Park in Kenya came across this female elephant gently carrying her dying infant into a sheltered spot in the forest. The mother and her three daughters remained with the baby for three days, long after it had died. Was it grief that kept them there?

Maybe it's easy to believe that chimpanzees feel grief because they seem to be so much like us. But what about birds? A young orphaned goose calls and calls for its parents. If it comes across an adult sleeping with its head tucked out of sight, it rushes up to it in greeting, thinking it might be a missing parent. When the adult bird shows its head, the youngster realizes its mistake and retreats.

A newborn porpoise, or any porpoise that needs help, is gently pushed to the surface by another porpoise so that it can breathe. Helping each other to the surface seems to come naturally to porpoises. But carrying a dead infant up to the surface and back again for days, as one female porpoise was seen doing, is not natural. Could it be grief that caused this mother porpoise's behavior?

Konrad Lorenz reported that the greylag geese he studied seemed to grieve upon the death of a mate. A grieving goose loses muscle tone, its eyes sink deep into their sockets and its head hangs low. The bird doesn't even defend itself when other geese challenge its position in the flock.

For the first three weeks of their lives, young peregrine falcons are protected and warmed by their mothers while their fathers hunt for food. But as the chicks grow, both parents must take turns hunting to provide them with enough food. In the sad event of one parent dying, it's often impossible for the remaining falcon to keep the chicks fed.

A peregrine falcon struggled for three days to feed five chicks after his mate was killed. Then he gave a strange cry and sat motionless for two days. By the time he began to hunt again, three of the chicks were dead, but by working nonstop he successfully raised the remaining two. Most scientists would say that he was simply acting on instinct. If he had tried to feed five chicks they all probably would have died. But the cry the falcon made just before he gave up hunting makes us want to believe he felt bad about sacrificing the weaker chicks so the stronger ones could live.

Do Animals Cry?

Every time you blink, your eyelids spread tears over the surface of your eyeball. Without a constant supply of tears, your eyes would quickly dry out and become easily infected. Animals keep their eyes moist with tears in the same way and for the same reason.

When you're hurt, you might suddenly produce more tears than normal in reaction to the pain. Some animals also have been seen crying when they are in painful situations. An elephant having a difficult time giving birth to her first calf was seen to cry. So was a gray parrot who was having trouble laying an egg.

It's possible that, like us, some animals cry from pain. But do they also cry when they're sad? Charles Darwin, the scientist who developed the theory of evolution, was convinced that Indian elephants cry tears of sadness. He wrote about some newly captured elephants that wept when they were tied up. And zookeepers occasionally report on captive elephants that cry when a longtime companion is taken away.

Hunters have long reported that seals cry when they see their young clubbed to death on the ice. But seals cry a lot of the time. Scientists think that a constant flow of cooling tears helps to prevent seals from overheating on land.

The tears that keep your eyes moist are the same as those you shed when you are hurt. But tears of sadness are different. They contain a special chemical that your brain produces to help you feel better. If animals produce this special type of tear, it would prove that they can feel sad. But until we know whether they do or not, we can only guess.

Look in the mirror at the inner corner of one of your eyes and you'll see tiny holes, called tear ducts, just like in this cat's eye. When your eyes water, the tear fluid drains into your tear ducts and then into your nose. That's why you have to blow your nose when you've been crying.

Don't Be Cruel

Animals kill for food and for living space, just like we do. But can they be cruel? When a cat hunts a mouse and plays with it before killing it, does the cat want to make the mouse suffer? Can it tell how frightened the mouse must be and feel pleasure knowing that? Probably not.

Experiments show that a cat goes on chasing, catching and killing mice long after it's stopped being hungry. After a while, it no longer kills them but continues to chase and catch them, then it stops catching them and only stalks them. What the cat gives up doing last — stalking mice — is a clue to what drives its behavior. Kitty might be your family pet, but first and foremost it's a hunter. And hunters often have to chase many animals before catching one, which might escape even then. Sometimes they have to catch more than they can eat, like when they're feeding a family.

So a cat is programmed to respond to anything that scampers away, including a ball of string that you yank across the floor. The cat is responding instinctively to a drive that tells it that, to survive, this is what it should do with little things that run away.

These mountain lion cubs are practicing pouncing on a tortoise. As they mature, their mother will bring small, live prey to the den so that the cubs can practice their hunting skills. If the tortoise pretends to be a rock, it can safely creep away when the cubs return to their den for a snooze.

A fox, like a wolf or a tiger, is a hunter whose survival depends on its skill and physical fitness. The look on this fox's face and the playful wagging of its tail show how much it enjoys using its lightning fast reflexes in a life-or-death game of tag. But the fox's main interest isn't torturing helpless mice, it's pouncing on little things that run away from it, because that's what its instinct tells it to do.

Foxes and other meat-eaters often kill more animals than they can eat so they can stash food away for hard times. Yet a fox will break into a henhouse, kill every chicken in sight and leave them all behind. Does it kill them for fun? Maybe it kills them because they surprise it by not running away. Or maybe the fox is simply enjoying exercising its own power, strength and speed. The more it kills, the more skillful it becomes at killing, and the better its chances of survival.

Shame on You

You probably know what it feels like to be ashamed of something you've done. Or maybe embarrassed by the clothes you have to wear to school. But can animals feel ashamed of their actions, or embarrassed by the way they look? Animals that are self-aware — like the chimps with the paint on their faces — might have these feelings. Even animals that aren't self-aware sometimes use body language that seems to say, "I'm so ashamed" — have you ever seen a dog that just had an accident on the best rug?

When a bottle-nosed dolphin called Wela accidentally bit her trainer's hand, she certainly looked as if she felt ashamed for what she'd done. Wela promptly dove to the bottom of the tank and stayed with her nose in a corner like a naughty child who's been punished for misbehaving in class. The dolphin refused to budge until her trainer swam down and coaxed her to the surface again.

Remember Alex, the African gray parrot you met on page 5? He makes a point of saying he's sorry whenever he bites his trainer. The fact that he goes ahead and bites her again suggests that his words don't really mean he regrets what he did. We often find ourselves apologizing for things we don't really feel sorry about, to be polite. Maybe some of his trainer's politeness has rubbed off on Alex.

"Dog," who never needed any other name, had such a thick, shaggy coat it made a warm bed for three barn cats on cold nights. Each summer the farmer clipped Dog's coat to make him more comfortable in the heat. But one summer, he gave Dog the shortest haircut of his life. Dog refused to leave his corner of the barn during daylight hours until his coat had regrown. Was he ashamed of his scrawny appearance? It certainly looked like it!

Scientists believe that there are times when feelings like shame or embarrassment might be useful for survival. They think that a form of shame makes sick Scottish red deer leave the herd. A sick deer stands out in the herd and can be quickly spotted by a predator. A deer that leaves the herd because of its sickly appearance will be more difficult to spot and will improve its chances of survival. But it's impossible to tell if the sick deer feels the embarrassment we would feel, or if it's merely following instinct.

A six-year-old chimp called Freud tried every way he could think of to get the attention of the leader of his troop. Leaping about and shaking branches had no effect, so he climbed a tall tree and set it swaying back and forth. Suddenly, it snapped, and down crashed Freud. After a quick glance to see if the leader had noticed, Freud crept away in embarrassment and busied himself with feeding.

Liar, Liar

Deception isn't exactly an emotion, but it goes hand-in-hand with strong feelings — guilt for telling a lie, fear of being caught and relief when you think you're getting away with it. To deceive someone, you must be aware that you know something they don't. And you must also understand how your behavior will affect them.

Researchers have discovered that rhesus monkeys can do all this. In one experiment, two boxes were fastened to the bars of the monkey enclosure. Both boxes contained sand and rocks, but one of them also contained peanuts. With the whole group together in the enclosure, only the top monkeys found the peanuts. But when the lower-ranking monkeys were tested separately, they quickly found the right box. It was obvious they weren't stupid. On the contrary, these clever monkeys knew their place in the group. It simply wouldn't do to appear to be as smart as their leaders.

It might not just be primates that recognize they know something others don't. If a raven (see below), which is a really smart bird, is caught hiding food it will dig it up and carry it to a new, secret site. Is the raven thinking to itself, "Uh-oh, I must find a better hiding place that only I know about"?

Jane Goodall reported seeing a wild male chimp named Mike take over command of his troop by bluffing. Being bossy and noisy are two requirements for the job of top chimp and Mike must have figured he needed some help to get the job. So he banged together a pair of empty kerosene cans to make more noise than he ever could with his voice. The racket he made with the cans while charging around helped him fool the troop into believing that he was the best — and loudest — chimp for the job!

Mike obviously knew how his behavior would affect his troop. But what about some of nature's biggest tricksters — birds? The female plover's most famous trick is to lure a predator away from her ground nest by faking a broken wing, which makes her look easy to catch. She might also pretend to be a mouse by crouching low then scurrying off making squeaking noises. Does the plover know what she's doing when she plays these tricks, or is she merely acting out of instinct?

Male and female gibbons are famous for singing duets. First one sings, then the other answers, and so on. The longer a gibbon couple stay together, the better they can defend their territory and the more practice they get singing together. But an intruder looking for new territory should listen carefully. A female that's recently lost her mate might be singing both parts of the duet to fool her neighbors into thinking her partner is still around helping her defend their patch of jungle.

No wonder we love dolphins so much. They're always smiling. They can't help it — their mouths are stuck that way. Researchers who work with them learn to tell how dolphins are feeling by watching what they do. Recognizing when a dolphin is excited isn't too difficult. But how do you know whether a dolphin, or any other animal, feels happy in the same way you do or looks forward to good things happening?

FEELING GOOD

Great Expectations

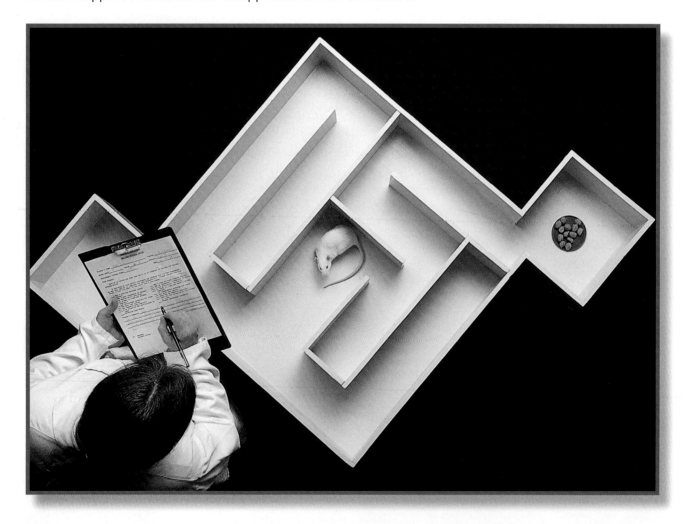

If fear is the feeling that something bad is about to happen, then hope is the feeling that something good might come your way. At 5:30 p.m. every day, our family dog reminds me it's dinnertime with the odd yodelling noises he makes when he wants something. When my dog's stomach is empty, he seems to have high hopes of being fed. And he's never been disappointed.

Many animal researchers report that animals act as if they're expecting something, and appear surprised or disappointed if it doesn't happen. Sometimes the disappointment can be intense.

Scientists set up experiments to see whether rats can find their way through complicated mazes for a food reward at the end. If the food isn't there after successful trials, the rats act confused and search everywhere for it. It seems that even rats experience hope. They expect a reward at the end of all their hard work. Wouldn't you?

In one experiment, a researcher placed a banana slice under one of two cups while a rhesus monkey watched. The researcher then hid the cups to test how long the monkey could remember which cup covered the banana. After the monkey started achieving perfect scores, the researcher switched the banana with a piece of lettuce. After searching unsuccessfully for the banana, the monkey turned and screamed angrily at the researcher. A piece of soggy lettuce definitely wasn't what this monkey was expecting!

Two months after Washoe the chimpanzee gave birth, her baby died, and her trainers thought it would be a good idea if she adopted another baby. When her trainers told Washoe that they had a baby for her, she excitedly used sign language to say "my baby." It seems as if she thought she was going to get her own baby back. Her hopes were disappointed when she saw the 10-month-old orphan chimp her trainers wanted her to adopt, and all her excitement disappeared. But soon she began playing with the baby and tried to rock him to sleep in her arms. By the next day, they were inseparable.

Chimps never fail to surprise us with their humanlike approach to life. They share food and care for others in their troops on the unspoken understanding that the others will return the favor later. If they don't, they're punished by the group. Do they act like this because they expect to be punished if they don't?

Jump for Joy

Cats' emotions can be difficult to read. Sometimes it's only a tail raised in greeting that lets you know a cat is happy to see you. Chimpanzees, however, leave little room for doubt. Kanzi, a young pygmy chimpanzee who was being trained to communicate with humans, hadn't seen his mother, Matata, for several weeks. One day, Kanzi's trainer told him there was a surprise for him in the next room — a "Matata surprise." Kanzi looked stunned, then ran to the door, gesturing impatiently for it to be opened. When he saw his mother, he leapt into her arms, and they screamed and hugged each other for a long time before breaking apart so they could gaze at each other. Then they laughed and played until they were exhausted.

In summertime, when food is abundant and the weather is mild, mountain goats can sometimes be seen doing a "war dance" on a snowbank high in the mountains. First one, then another, bucks and twirls, kicking and sliding through the snow. Eventually, the whole band joins in, dancing — or so it seems — just for the joy of living.

How can we tell if animals feel pleasure the way we do? One researcher found a way. He offered sugar water to rats and humans before and after they'd eaten, then plotted on a graph how much sugar water the rats drank. Next he asked the humans whether an empty or a full stomach affected how they felt about the taste of sugar water, and plotted their responses on a separate graph. When he compared the two graphs he was startled to find that they were almost identical. Rats react in the same way towards the taste of sweetness as humans say they do, which could mean that they feel the same way about it as humans do. Sometimes it's a pleasure to drink something sweet. Other times, it's not.

Many dolphins and porpoises are accidentally caught in tuna nets each year. Some of them manage to escape by waiting until part of the net dips below the surface. As soon as they're free, these intelligent mammals leap repeatedly into the air. Are they jumping for joy?

Love and Kisses

Human parents love their children. Their words and their actions say they do. Yet underneath all that tender, loving care is a strong instinct for survival. It has to do with making sure that part of us lives on in future generations of our family. What lives on are our genes — coded instructions that tell all the cells in our bodies how and when to grow, and what shape and size to grow. If your nose looks like your grandma's and your hair like your dad's, it's proof that their genes live on in you. All animals share this instinct for the survival of their genes, including the wolf spider (see opposite page). We accept caring behavior in humans as proof that they love their children, but we think similar behavior in a spider is proof that it's acting out of the instinct to preserve its own genes.

Like most human, monkey and ape mothers, this Japanese macaque cradles her infant on her left. Is it so her baby can hear the reassuring sounds of her heartbeats? Apparently not. She holds her infant on the left so that it's closest to her left eye and ear. Why? Because the left eye and ear are controlled by the right side of the brain — the side that specializes in interpreting emotions. By choosing their left side, most primate mothers can quickly tune in to how their baby is feeling.

Unfortunately, it's difficult to come up with an experiment that will prove spider mothers act out of love. Female rats, however, demonstrated very clearly in one experiment that they were even prepared to cross over an electrified grid to rescue abandoned baby rats. One female rescued 58 babies, cramming them all into her nest. Why would this rat try to save babies that weren't her own if she were merely acting out of an instinct to preserve her own genes?

A female Japanese macaque wailed for hours when her baby died. Eventually, an older female arrived and comforted her. She was the baby's grandmother, who lived some distance away. She hadn't seen her daughter for years, but when she recognized her daughter's anguished cry for help there was only one thing to do: find her and give her the big, comforting hug she so obviously needed.

Being a wolf spider mom can be back-breaking work. She lays as many as 100 eggs, then keeps them safe by carrying them around on her back for weeks. Even when they hatch into spiderlings, she carries them around until they know enough to survive on their own. And if she comes across any orphan wolf spiderlings, she'll look after them, too. Sounds like love, but is it?

How Do Animals Show Their Feelings?

For many years a scientist named David Macdonald studied wild foxes. He raised captive foxes to learn about their family life. One autumn he introduced a dog (or male) fox called Smudge to three vixens (or females) called Whitepaws (the boss), Big Ears and Wide Eyes. The sisters became rivals when Smudge chose Whitepaws as his mate. Whitepaws would attack Wide Eyes, and both her sisters constantly tried to force Smudge to notice them.

When Whitepaws had cubs, Smudge started to bring food to the den and bury what wasn't eaten. He and Big Ears could visit the cubs, but Whitepaws banned Wide Eyes. Soon Big Ears began to babysit the cubs, acting like a disapproving aunt and scolding Smudge for playing too hard with them. Smudge would skulk off and wait for Big Ears to fall asleep. Then he'd quietly call for his cubs and they'd sneak out to play with him. It wasn't until the cubs were eating solid food that Whitepaws finally let Wide Eyes near them.

If Whitepaws, Smudge, Big Ears and Wide Eyes were people instead of foxes, we'd recognize all kinds of emotions behind their actions — jealousy, friendship, love, concern for others, even deceit. But they're not, so we can't be sure. What David Macdonald is sure he recognizes, however, is the body language that foxes use to show what they are feeling.

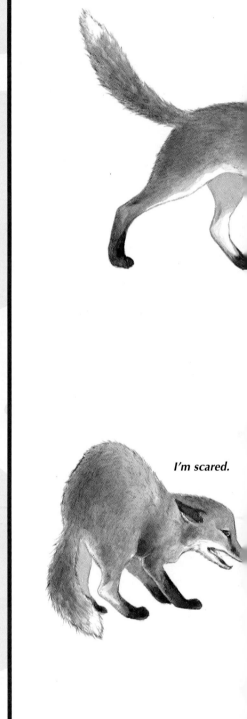

I'm scared.

Imagine That!

Have you ever seen something so beautiful that it fills you with awe? Or felt chills go down your spine when you hear a piece of music you love? It might be that humans aren't the only creatures affected emotionally by beauty and music. A research student at the Gombe Reserve in Africa reported seeing two chimpanzees hand in hand, on top of a ridge before a beautiful sunset. They might have had another reason for sitting there, but it's nice to imagine they were enjoying the view. Another researcher discovered that chickens seem to react emotionally to the music of Pink Floyd, ruffling their feathers and moving around. And Michael, a gorilla who uses sign language, loves to listen to opera star Luciano Pavarotti.

We believe that one of the big differences between humans and animals is that we can create things that express our emotions, and animals can't. But it seems art and imagination might not be strictly human. Several years ago, an expert on abstract art at Syracuse University in New York State was asked for his opinion on the work of a new, unknown artist. The expert thought the abstract drawings were very beautiful and graceful, full of energy and emotion. He concluded that they were probably the work of a female artist who was interested in the art of Asian handwriting. He was right about the artist being female, and he got the Asian connection right. What he didn't know was that the artist was an Asian *elephant* called Siri!

Meet Charles, a silverback gorilla at the Metropolitan Toronto Zoo who's wild about painting. Charles discovered how much fun painting was after keepers let him experiment with some finger paints. In fact, he loves experimenting so much he often works on three paintings at once! Charles even signs his paintings — with either a fingerprint or his handprint.

Lincoln Park Zoo in Chicago is home to a famous chimpanzee artist called June, who has even had a one-chimp show at a Chicago art gallery. Kiri is a young chimp that's following in June's footsteps. But unlike June, who hates getting paint on her hands, young Kiri really throws himself into his work.

Humans love horror movies, because it's fun to make ourselves scared when there isn't any real danger. Can animals enjoy imagining danger, too? Panbanisha is a pygmy chimpanzee who loves to pretend there's a monster in the next room. Her hair stands on end as she approaches the door and signs "monster." Sometimes Panbanisha puts on a monster mask and chases her sister Tamuli. Two other chimps, Austin and Sherman, were watching the movie *King Kong* on television. There was a cage in their room that looked just like the one on television, and they both began to pretend that King Kong was in there. The game became so real to them that both chimps stopped watching the television and began to bark at the cage and throw things at it. Sherman even got out the water hose and sprayed the cage.

Many elephants, both in captivity and in the wild, have been seen scratching designs in the dirt. Some scientists think this raises an interesting question about how we developed our own artistic abilities. If, as some believe, early humans developed an ear for music by listening to the songs of birds, is it possible that they learned to draw by watching ancient elephants doodling in the dirt?

Koko the gorilla was grief-stricken when her pet kitten All Ball died. Scientists are discovering that some animals, especially very social animals, are capable of showing concern for others. Some even go beyond their immediate families and friends and show concern for animals of other species.

FEELING FOR OTHERS

Let's Be Friends

Can animals be friends? Scientists don't like to use words like friendship when it comes to animals. While we're ready to believe that animals experience hostile emotions like anger, we seem to reserve the "good" ones for ourselves. But can we accept that animals can have rivals and not consider that they can do the opposite and have friends? And if animals act in loving ways towards their own young, is it possible that they do the same for unrelated animals?

Even animals of different species have become friends. Donkeys have formed strong bonds with goats (see below) as well as with horses. Wild chimps have been seen getting along with baboons and other primates (opposite, a chimp and mandrill). And dogs and cats can become the best of friends.

Frans de Waal, who has studied primates for many years, reported how a female chimpanzee called Atlanta became friends with a younger chimp called Mai, who was giving birth to a baby. When the baby was born, Atlanta screamed and hugged two nearby chimpanzees in excitement. The next day, she fiercely defended the new mother in a fight. She frequently groomed Mai and spent time gazing at her baby and gently touching it.

Researchers witnessed a female Rodrigues fruit bat helping an unrelated bat who was having trouble giving birth. The "midwife" bat groomed the mother-to-be, tried to keep her cool by fanning her and repeatedly showed her the best position to give birth. Other bats also tried to help. One fanned the mother with her wings, while a male bat tried to protect the mother by placing himself between her and the researchers who were watching.

The Royal Society for the Prevention of Cruelty to Animals (RSPCA) in England recently took care of a goat called Rainbow and a calf called Locksley that became friends at first sight. Fortunately, the society was able to find them a home where they could stay together.

Crows are known for looking after each other when they're sick. One male crow was seen to bring food regularly to a lone, partly blind female crow. He didn't just do it once, or several times. He did it consistently through two whole breeding seasons, even though he was also working hard with his mate to provide food for a nestful of chicks. Why would this crow go out of his way to help a bird that couldn't return the favor? Was she related to him? Or was he acting purely out of friendship?

Let Me Help

Animals that live in complex social groups sometimes act in friendly ways towards animals who aren't related at all, even animals that belong to another species. Is it possible that these animals go beyond instinct and help strangers when there's no advantage to them?

This might explain the actions of a group of chimpanzees at Basel Zoo in Switzerland after a sparrow crash-landed in their enclosure. When one chimp scooped up the terrified bird, the keeper expected the worst. But the chimp gently cradled the bird in her hand and gazed at it. Soon the other chimps gathered around to see what she held. Then very carefully, the bird was passed from chimp to chimp until the last chimp walked to the bars of the enclosure and handed it delicately to the, by now, astounded keeper.

Koko showed such tenderness to her kitten All Ball that her trainer Francine Patterson gave her a new kitten when All Ball died. Soon Koko and her new kitten, which she named Smoky, became inseparable. Has the experience of being raised by humans helped Koko and other animals to develop more feelings for other species than they would have naturally in the wild?

And then there's Koko the gorilla, who offered a woman visitor orange juice after she complained of a sick stomach. The next time they met, Koko asked in sign language if she'd like more juice. But was she doing it out of concern for the woman's health? Some scientists believe that chimps and gorillas are so tuned in to each other's thoughts, feelings and preferences, they are the world's "natural psychologists." But other scientists disagree. Maybe the chimps in Basel Zoo were just curious. And maybe Koko was just showing how smart she was to remember that the woman drank orange juice the first time they met.

When a three-year-old boy fell into the gorilla pit in a zoo just out-side Chicago, the crowd watched horror-struck as a large gorilla raced over to the child. But their horror soon turned to amazement. The female gorilla carefully picked up the child and cuddled him, then carried him to the entrance of the gorilla enclosure so that the keeper could take him back to his parents. The gorilla was related to Koko, and was also raised and trained by humans her whole life.

Animal Heroes

We've long thought that humans are the only creatures capable of acting in a completely unselfish way — helping others at a sacrifice to themselves. But there are plenty of stories that suggest animals show generosity, even bravery, in the way they come to the aid of others. Like Old Man, for instance, a chimp who lived in a Florida zoo and who became friends with his keeper. One day the other chimps became frightened and attacked the keeper, and Old Man rushed to his defense even though he risked injury himself. Would you say Old Man acted bravely, even though some researchers claim that chimps aren't as sensitive to pain as you are?

In the spring of 1996 a cat called Scarlet risked her life to carry her four-week-old kittens one by one from a burning New York building. By the time they were all safe, Scarlet's eyes were blistered shut and her paws were burned. The only way she could reassure herself they were all accounted for was to touch each one with her nose.

To survive, a vampire bat needs to drink half its own weight in blood each night. It finds a sleeping cow or horse, then uses its sharp teeth to carefully shave away a little patch of skin so it can lap up the blood that oozes to the surface. This can take 20 minutes, and an inexperienced bat might be shaken off before it has a chance to finish feeding. Two nights without blood spells death to a vampire bat. When female vampire bats return to the roost after feeding, they bring up some of the blood they've drunk and give it to their pups. They will also give some of their precious food supply to hungry adults. Astonishingly, they feed not just relatives, but any adult that's in danger of starving.

Jim Gilchrist certainly thinks his dogs are heroes. One winter's day, Jim and his rottweiler, Tara, fell through the ice on Lake Simcoe, Ontario. As Jim and Tara struggled in the water his golden retriever, Tiree, without any urging, crawled across the ice so that Jim could grab his collar. Next Tara scrambled up onto the ice next to Tiree so that Jim could grab her collar too. Then both dogs slowly hauled Jim out of the water by clawing their way backwards on the ice. What prompted both dogs to risk their lives for their owner? Could it be unselfish love?

Four-year-old Tara (left) and one-year-old Tiree (right) were inducted into the Purina Animal Heroes Hall of Fame after they saved their owner, Jim Gilchrist, when he plunged into the icy waters of Lake Simcoe.

42

Adult vampire bats share their food with other bats when they have found blood to feed on. Of course, it works both ways. A bat that feeds successfully tonight might not be so lucky tomorrow. But at least she knows that she can rely on her neighbors to keep her alive. Is this generosity — or instinctive behavior to preserve the group?

Do Animals Have Rights?

We don't know whether animals suffer the same way we do because they can't tell us how they feel. But the fact that animals can't raise their own voices to protest being locked up in zoos, bred in factory farms and experimented on in laboratories doesn't mean that we don't need to think carefully about what we do to them.

What can you do to treat animals fairly? Try to find out whether the meat and eggs you eat come from factory farms that use cruel farming methods. Check if the tests to make sure your shampoo, toothpaste and other household products are safe for you to use were done on animals. If enough people refuse to buy food and products that involve cruelty to animals, supermarkets and stores will find new suppliers who use kinder ways to raise farm animals and test products.

After the film Free Willy, *many people demanded that its star, Keiko (below), be set free. As a first step toward this goal, he was moved to Oregon, where he was nursed back to health and taught about being a killer whale. If he can hunt for himself when he's moved to a fenced-off area of a fjord in the North Atlantic, he stands a chance of surviving in the wild. But will he be able to live a normal life with other killer whales? Alas, no one knows.*

Releasing zoo animals that have been captive for many years won't solve their problems. Most of them lack the skills needed to survive in the wild. Instead, many zoos are now helping their animals to live more natural and more fulfilling lives. Perhaps the zoo as we know it today is on its way out, to be replaced by conservation zoos that help endangered species to survive. Find out what plans your local zoo has for the future.

Chickens hate squeezing through really tight spaces. Yet in a series of amazing experiments designed to discover what chickens consider really important in their lives, time after time chickens squeezed through a tight space to reach a nesting box in which to lay their eggs. Chickens raised in factory farms are expected to lay eggs every day of their lives without so much as a glimpse of a nesting box.

Animals Up Close

It's difficult knowing what an animal is feeling, but you can become more sensitive to animals so that you can tune in to their lives and understand them a little better. If you or a friend have a pet, you can learn about its feelings and needs by watching how it acts and reacts to what you do. As you become a better observer you'll recognize that a pet uses body language and sounds — some surprisingly like your own — to let you know how it's feeling.

Most people feed their cat by putting down a dish of food then walking away from it. When a mother cat catches a bird or a mouse for her kittens, she too puts it on the ground and then walks away to show that it's all theirs. No wonder cats think humans who feed them in this way must be their mothers!

The key to understanding a pet is to try to see things from its point of view. A puppy's life, like that of a wolf cub or fox kit, revolves around its pack, and it has to figure out its position in it. By watching carefully, the puppy learns which members of its human pack it has to avoid upsetting and which ones it can play with or try to boss around. What it usually learns is that it's the most junior member of the pack and will likely stay that way. That's why fully grown dogs continue to act like puppies, always ready to play and ready also to roll onto their backs to show the leader of their human pack that they know who's boss.

A dog might treat you like the leader of the pack but to a cat you'll always be Mom. Ever wondered why a cat climbs onto your lap for a cuddle and before long starts to purr loudly and knead you with its front paws? Perhaps the comforting, soft curve of your lap confuses it into thinking it's a kitten again, snuggled close to its mother. When kittens want a drink of milk, all they have to do is knead their mother's breast and purr to make her milk flow.

One day we might know for certain whether animals feel emotions in the same way we do. Until we do, we should give them the benefit of the doubt and treat all animals kindly. And there's no better place to start being kind to animals than in our own homes.

If someone were to give you a new puppy would you know how to make it happy? Here's how: let your puppy know that it belongs to its new human pack by giving it a cozy place to sleep and helping it learn the daily rhythm of its new pack. Try to feed, groom and walk your puppy at the same times each day, and give it plenty of opportunities to play with other dogs. Having to use dog manners, communicate with dogs and learn dog customs will remind your puppy that it really is a dog, even if it belongs to a pack of humans.

Index